Scale Studies

(One String)

for the Viola

Part One

One-Octave
Scales

by Cassia Harvey

CHP341

©2018 by C. Harvey Publications All Rights Reserved.
www.charveypublications.com

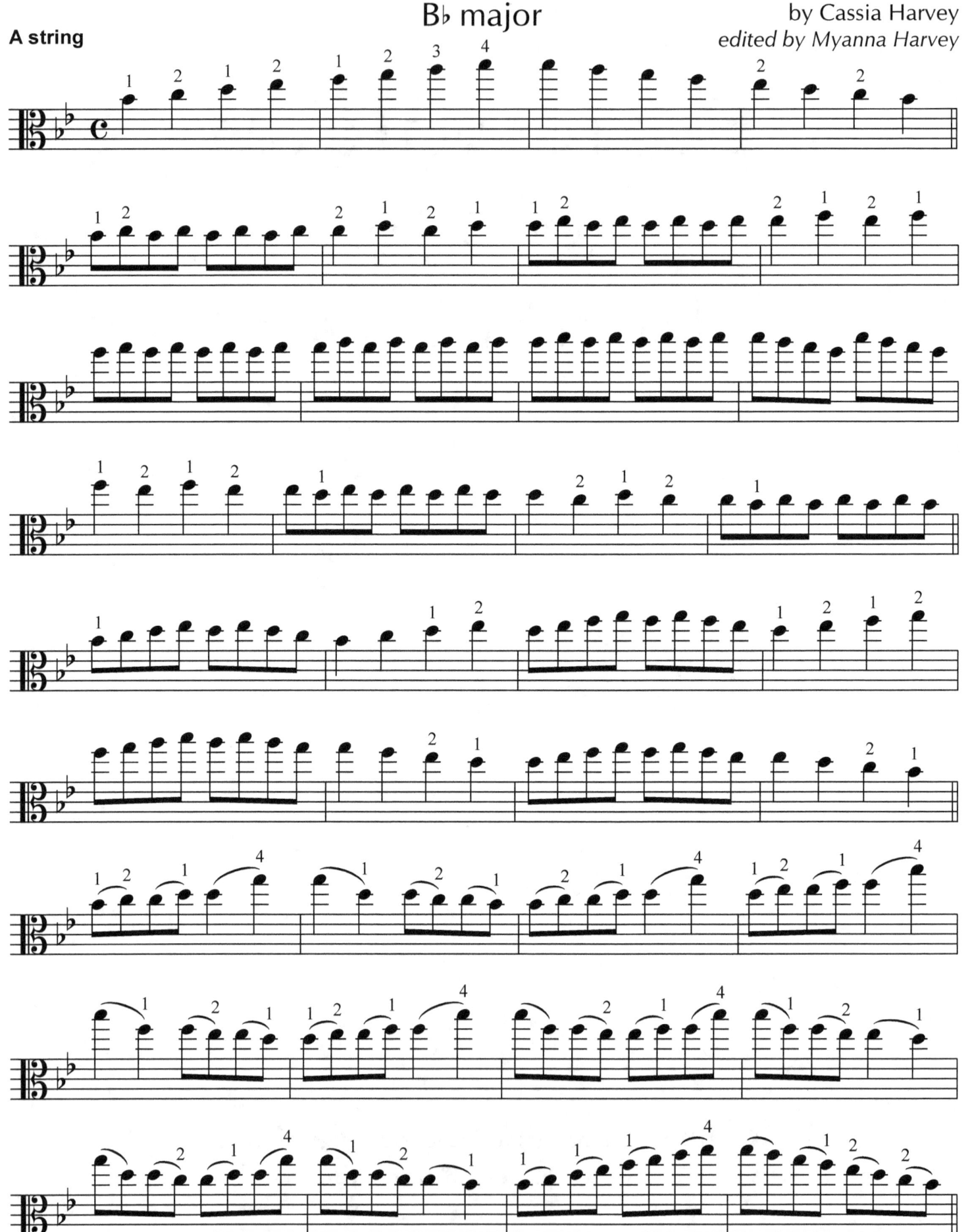

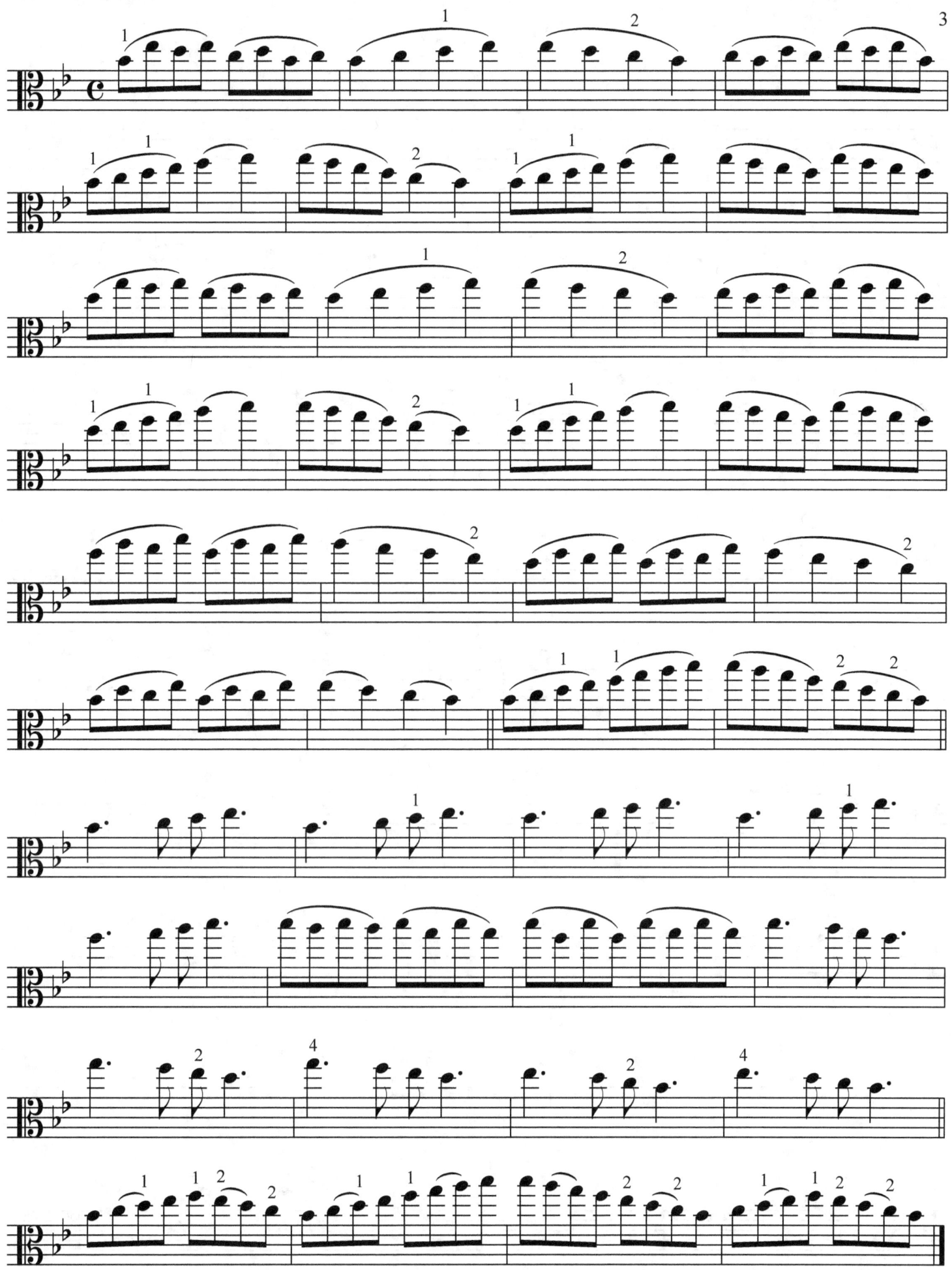

Scale Studies (One String) for the Viola, Part One: One-Octave Scales

E♭ major

D string

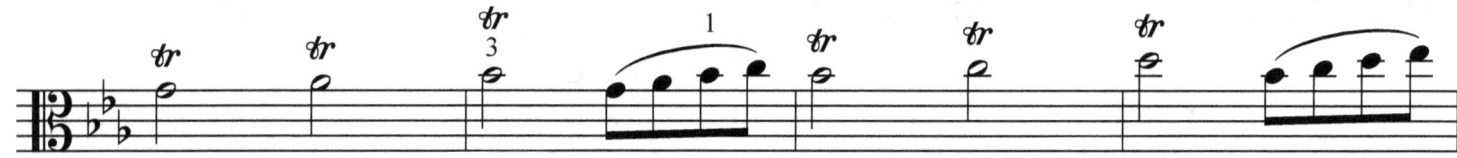

Scale Studies (One String) for the Viola, Part One: One-Octave Scales © 2018 C. Harvey Publications All Rights Reserved.

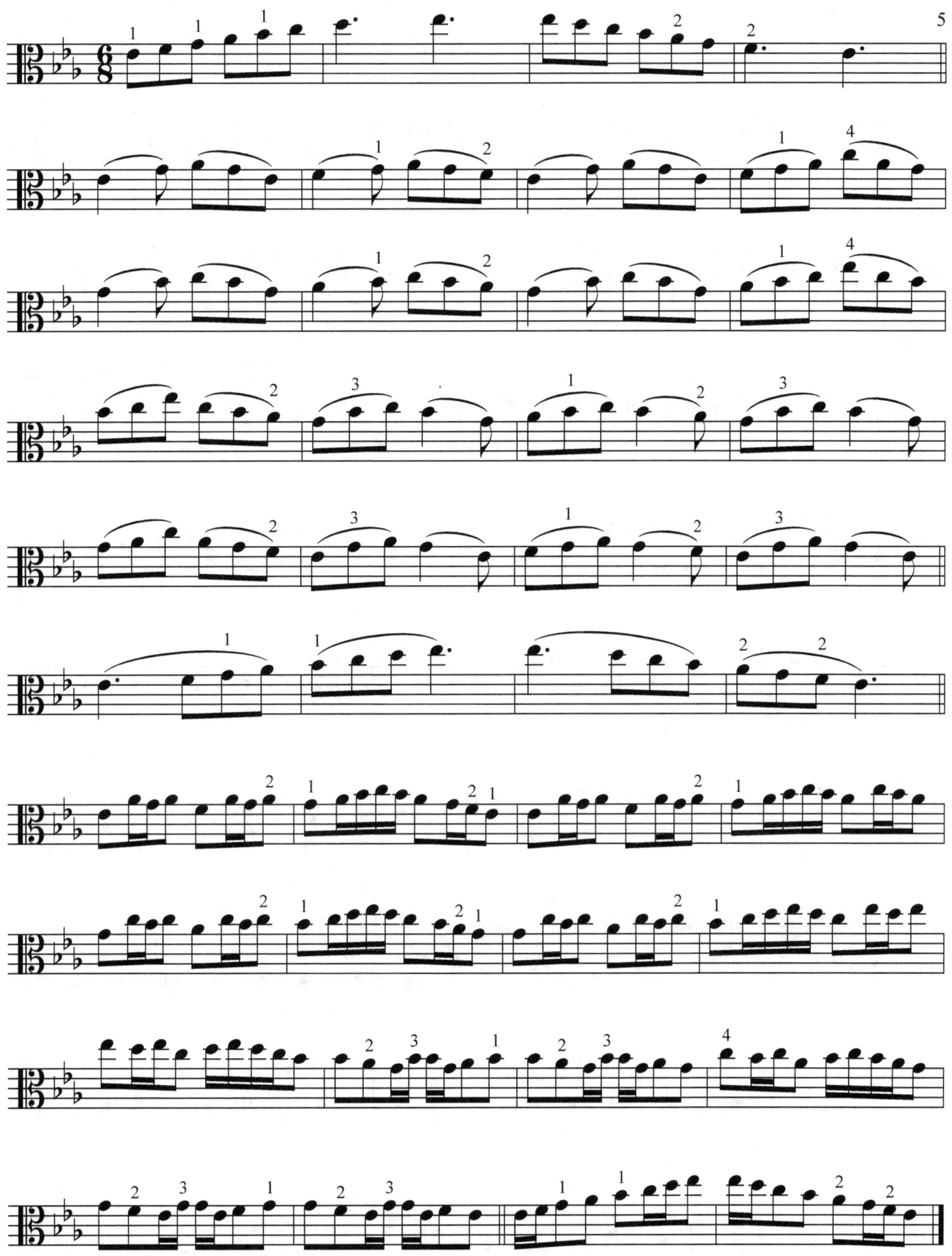

A♭ major

G string

Scale Studies (One String) for the Viola, Part One: One-Octave Scales ©2018 C. Harvey Publications All Rights Reserved.

Scale Studies (One String) for the Viola, Part One: One-Octave Scales

©2018 C. Harvey Publications All Rights Reserved.

D♭ major

C string

Scale Studies (One String) for the Viola, Part One: One-Octave Scales ©2018 C. Harvey Publications All Rights Reserved.

Scale Studies (One String) for the Viola, Part One: One-Octave Scales ©2018 C. Harvey Publications All Rights Reserved.

B♭ major

A string

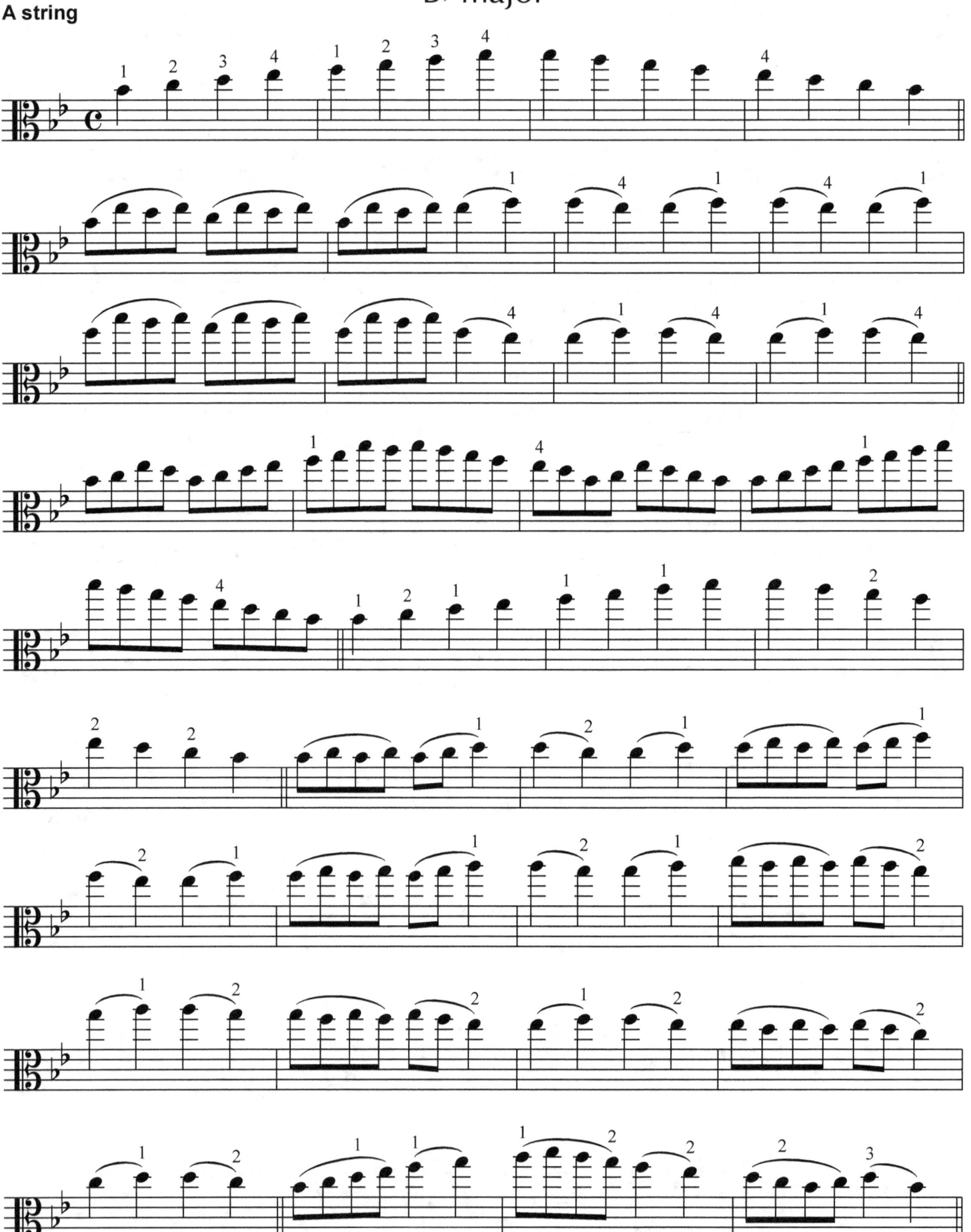

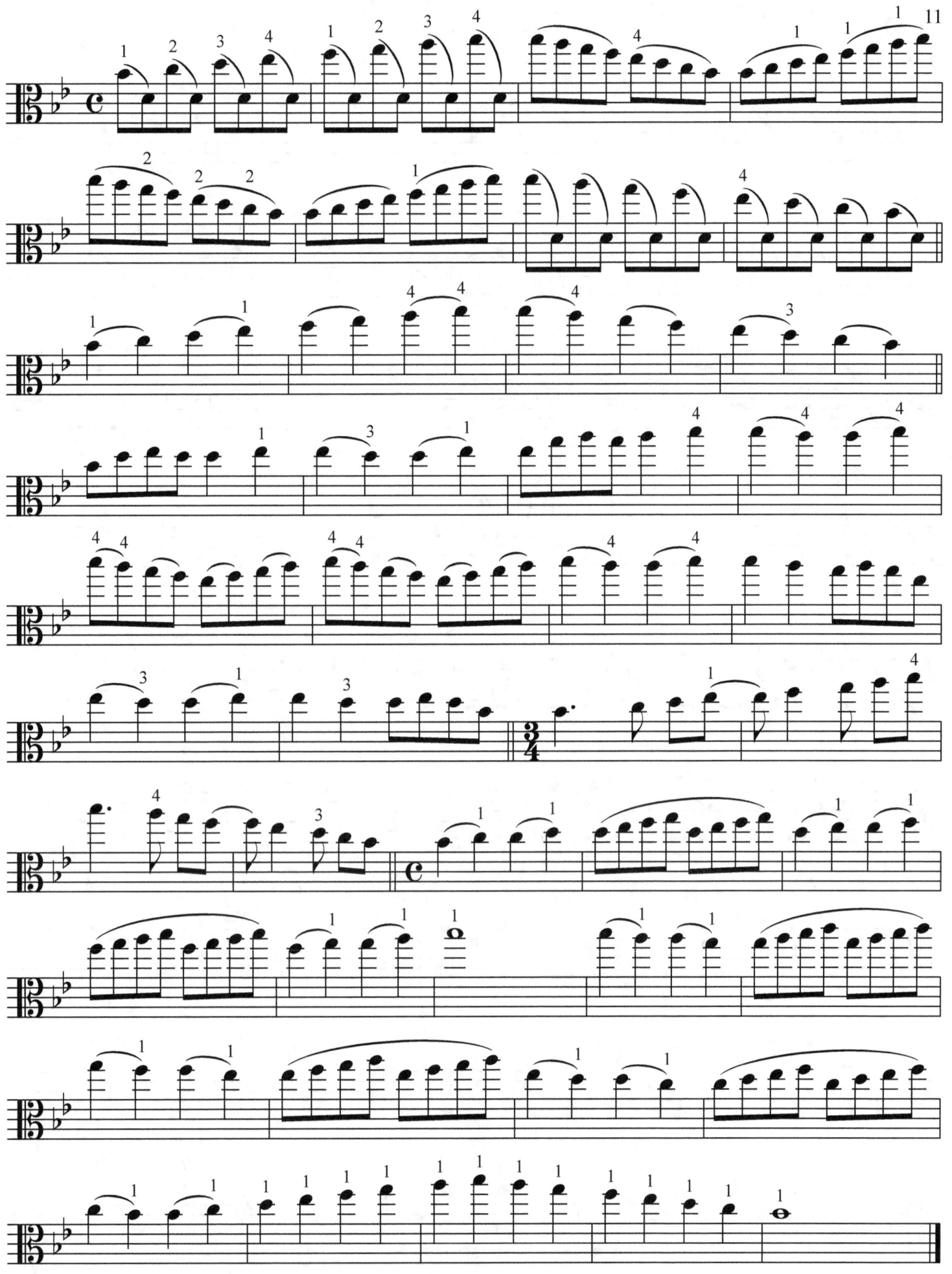

Scale Studies (One String) for the Viola, Part One: One-Octave Scales ©2018 C. Harvey Publications All Rights Reserved.

Scale Studies (One String) for the Viola, Part One: One-Octave Scales ©2018 C. Harvey Publications All Rights Reserved.

A♭ major

G string

Scale Studies (One String) for the Viola, Part One: One-Octave Scales ©2018 C. Harvey Publications All Rights Reserved.

Scale Studies (One String) for the Viola, Part One: One-Octave Scales ©2018 C. Harvey Publications All Rights Reserved.

D♭ major

C string

Scale Studies (One String) for the Viola, Part One: One-Octave Scales

Scale Studies (One String) for the Viola, Part One: One-Octave Scales ©2018 C. Harvey Publications All Rights Reserved.

B major

A string

Scale Studies (One String) for the Viola, Part One: One-Octave Scales ©2018 C. Harvey Publications All Rights Reserved.

Scale Studies (One String) for the Viola, Part One: One-Octave Scales ©2018 C. Harvey Publications All Rights Reserved.

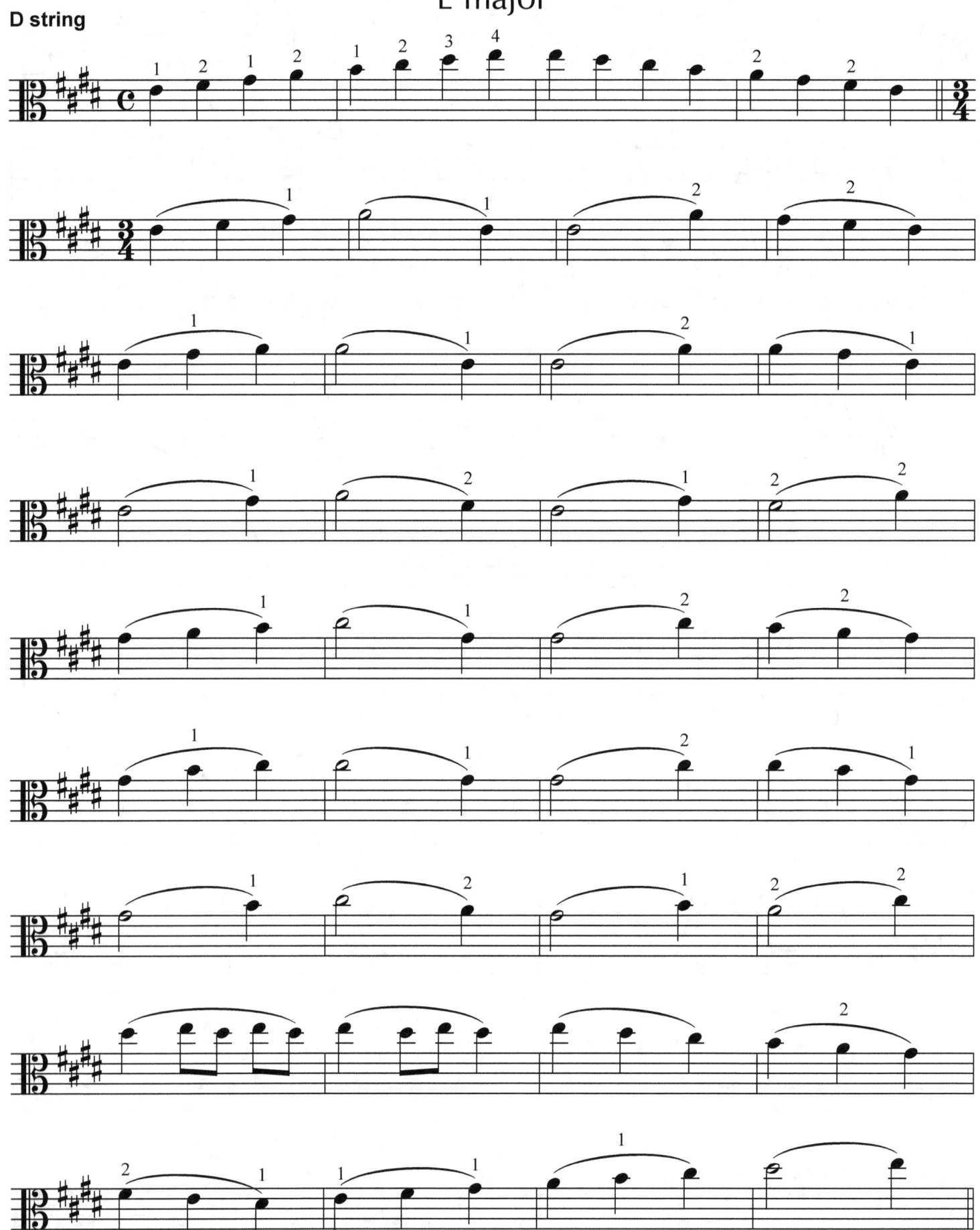

Scale Studies (One String) for the Viola, Part One: One-Octave Scales ©2018 C. Harvey Publications All Rights Reserved.

A major

G string

Scale Studies (One String) for the Viola, Part One: One-Octave Scales

©2018 C. Harvey Publications All Rights Reserved.

D major

C string

Scale Studies (One String) for the Viola, Part One: One-Octave Scales ©2018 C. Harvey Publications All Rights Reserved.

B harmonic minor

A string

Scale Studies (One String) for the Viola, Part One: One-Octave Scales ©2018 C. Harvey Publications All Rights Reserved.

E harmonic minor

D string

A harmonic minor

G string

B melodic minor

A string

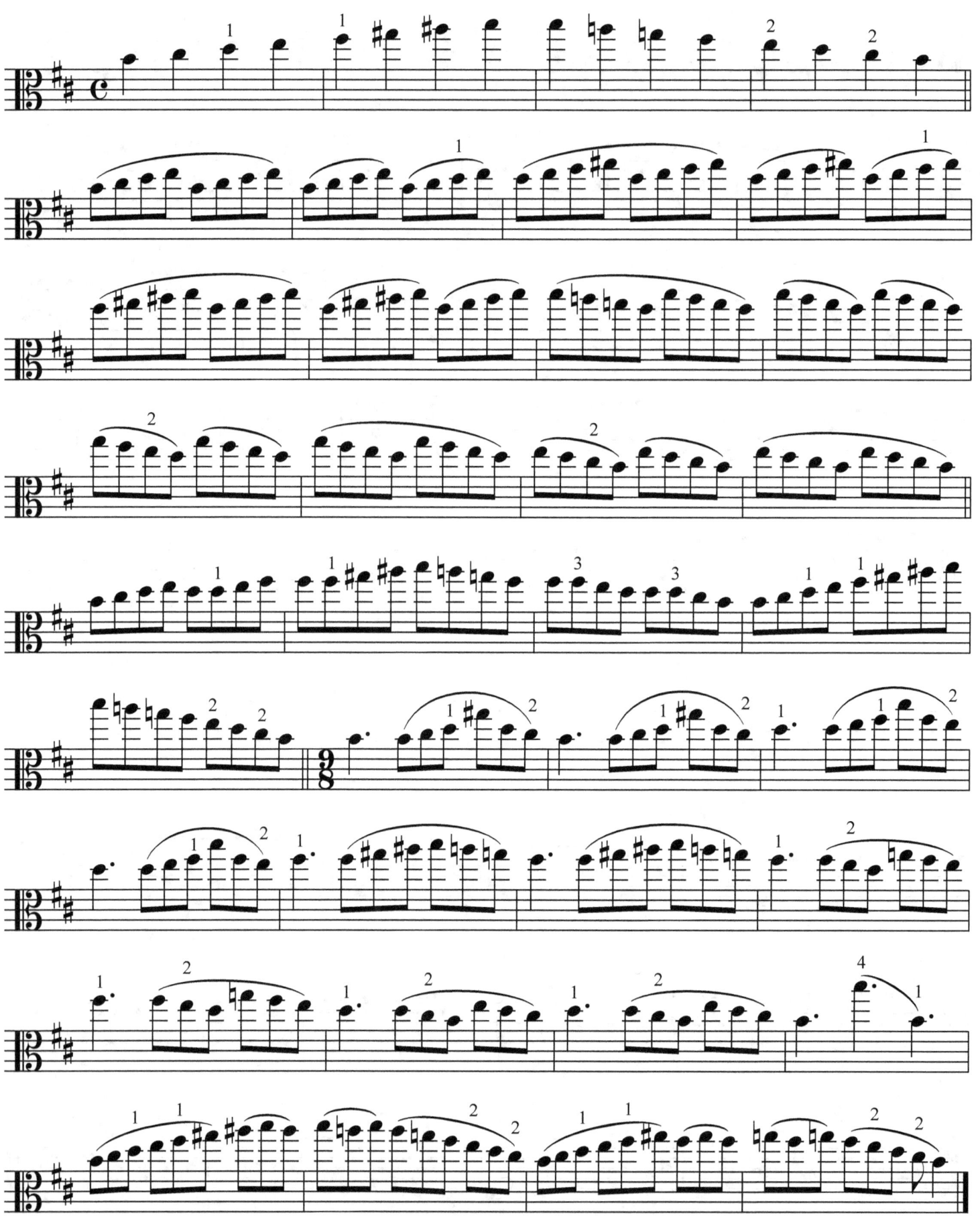

Scale Studies (One String) for the Viola, Part One: One-Octave Scales

E melodic minor

D string

Scale Studies (One String) for the Viola, Part One: One-Octave Scales

A melodic minor

G string

Scale Studies (One String) for the Viola, Part One: One-Octave Scales

D melodic minor

C string

also available from www.charveypublications.com: CHP323

Finger Exercises for the Viola, Book Two

1

Low First Finger

Cassia Harvey

©2018 C. Harvey Publications All Rights Reserved.

www.ingramcontent.com/pod-product-compliance
Lightning Source LLC
Chambersburg PA
CBHW051429070526
44584CB00023B/3640